# BOSTON
## History, People, Landmarks

FENWAY PARK, BOSTON COMMON, PAUL REVERE

TAMRA B. ORR

CURIOUS
FOX
BOOKS

Paperback ISBN 979-8-89094-044-5
Hardcover ISBN 979-8-89094-045-2

Library of Congress Control Number: 2023943818

To learn more about the other great books from Fox Chapel Publishing, or to find a retailer near you, call toll-free 800-457-9112 or visit us at *www.FoxChapelPublishing.com*.

We are always looking for talented authors. To submit an idea, please send a brief inquiry to acquisitions@foxchapelpublishing.com.

Fox Chapel Publishing makes every effort to use environmentally friendly paper for printing.

Printed in China

**ABOUT THE AUTHOR:** Tamra B. Orr is a full-time author. She has written more than 500 educational books for readers of all ages. A graduate of Ball State University in Muncie, Indiana, Orr is a mother of four, an avid letter writer, and a travel enthusiast! She loves to hop in the car for long road trips, and heading east to Boston was one of her favorite adventures.

# BOSTON

- Boston, Massachusetts
- 25th largest city in the USA
- 89.6 square miles
- Population: 675,647
- Elevation: 46 ft.
- Settled: 1625

People in the city
are known as
**"Bostonians"**

Best known as a birthplace of the American Revolution and a host of one of the most famous marathons in the world, Boston is also a center for education and innovation, a modern city filled with living history, and a home for millions of varied and close-knit communities representing cultural heritage from around the world.

Thousands of people come to the city every year to learn at renowned Harvard University or the groundbreaking Massachusetts Institute of Technology. Tourists come to discover history at spots like the Boston Tea Party Ships & Museum or via walking tours like the Black Heritage Trail. They explore the vast cultural landscape of the city through the many museums, heritage festivals, and parades in the city.

It's a city with a rich history, breathtaking sites, and delicious seafood—welcome to Boston!

# CONTENTS

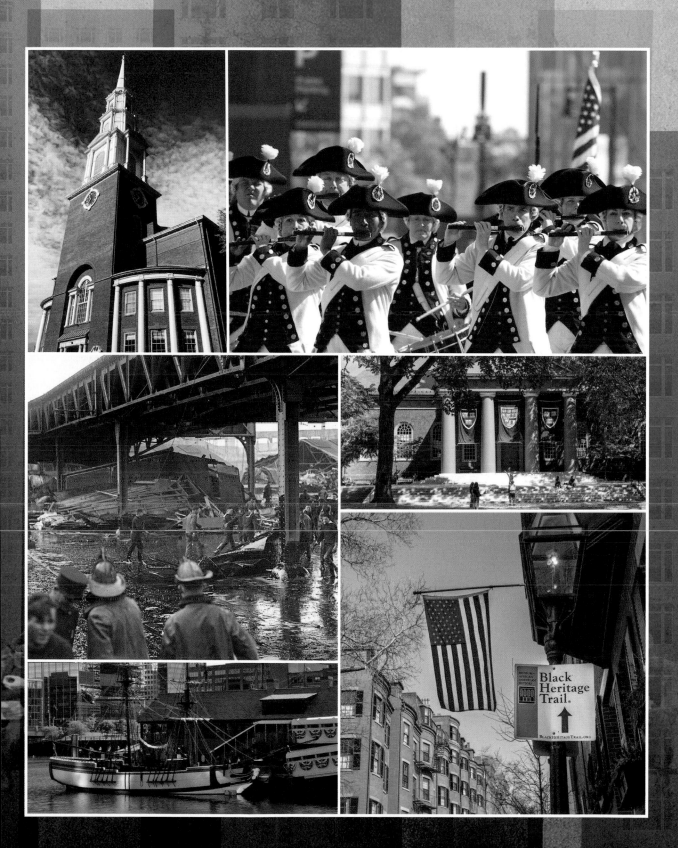

Every year, tourists and locals watch Boston Marathon runners wind through the city.

# "On Your Mark"

At just after noon on a spring day in April 1897, fifteen men stood at the starting line. They tried hard to be patient. Most had arrived in Boston early that morning by train and had been waiting for hours. Now they stretched, working to warm up and loosen their muscles as the crowd around them grew restless. Everyone was waiting for the event to begin. No one there could have had any idea that they were about to start a Boston tradition that would last for more than a century.

At last, at 12:19 p.m., the starter said the golden word: "Go!" The men all surged forward. The first Boston Marathon had begun.

One of the men who had helped organize the U.S. marathon team for the Olympics, John Graham, along with local businessman Herbert Holton, had brought the race to Boston. They decided to hold it on Patriots' Day. This holiday, celebrated in Massachusetts and Maine, honors the start of the Revolutionary War.

As the minutes and the miles passed, the runners focused on pacing themselves. The 24.5 mile route ran from Metcalf's Mill in Ashland to Boston's Irving Street Oval near Copley Square. It had uneven ground, curves, and hills. As the men ran, they had constant company. Soldiers rode bicycles alongside each man, ready to hand out water, lemons, or wet handkerchiefs. They were also there to help anyone who got hurt—or gave up before the finish line.

### Chapter One

**Fred S. Cameron wins the Boston Marathon in 1910.**

The hardest part of the run was, without question, Heartbreak Hill. Located between miles 20 and 21, it was not terribly high at only about 91 feet, but it had a very steep rise. By the time the runners reached it, they were also usually quite tired. The hill got it's name during the 1936 marathon. As the story goes, runner Johnny Kelley passed his top rival, Tarzan Brown. As he ran by, he patted him on the back. Brown

**In 2016, runners make the same trip.**

was so upset he powered through and won the race. When a *Boston Globe* reporter wrote about the moment in the newspaper, he stated that losing "broke Kelley's heart." A nickname was born—"Heartbreak Hill"—and it stuck.

New Yorker John J. McDermott won the first Boston marathon. Since then, it has been held every year for more than a century. There have been many changes since that day in 1897. In 1924, the course was lengthened to 26.2 miles.  In 1975, a wheelchair division was added to the race. While only 15 men participated in the first race, today the event attracts more than 30,000 people of all genders. If you're at least 18 years old and can run the distance within a set qualifying range (around 3–5 hours, depending on your age bracket), you can apply to run in the race!

During the 2013 Marathon, there was a terrorist bombing. Three people were killed and more than 300 were injured. Instead of  scaring people away from the event, however, the following year the race had more participants than ever. This perseverance and spirit is part of what continues to make the race so beloved around the world.

**John J. McDermott was the first winner of the Boston Marathon. He ran again in 1898 and came in fourth.**

Above: Algonquin homes were some of the first structures built in New England. Left: Captain John Smith was one of the first Europeans to arrive in New England.

# The Fight for Independence

The first people to live in the area of the future Boston were Native Americans. In 2400 BCE, most lived on a peninsula called Shawmut. The exact meaning of the name is uncertain, but it's thought to be something like "the place of clear waters." The peninsula was made up of rolling hills at this time, including Mount Vernon, Beacon Hill, and Pemberton Hill. One day settlers would refer to these three as the Trimount. Development during the Industrial Revolution would see this area turned into a wide, flat landmass, but for now it was a narrow, hilly strip. By 1600 CE, almost 100,000 Algonquin lived throughout what would one day be New England.

In the early seventeenth century, some of the first Europeans sailed down the coast of these lands. Soldier and explorer Captain John Smith led the expedition. For more than two years, Smith mapped the northeast coast. To make it sound more inviting to possible colonists, the British captain called the region New England. He named the southern river (in Massachusetts) Charles, in honor of England's Prince Charles. He called the northern one (in Maine) the Kennebec River after the bay it flows into. *Kennebec* means "bay" in the Abenaki language.

As more Europeans came to explore this area, they brought along new types of food and weapons—and new illnesses. In 1617, a smallpox epidemic came ashore with these explorers. Within a year,

**After Blaxton moved from this house on Beacon Hill, 44 acres of his land became Boston Common.**

almost 90 percent of the Native Americans had died. More epidemics swept through in 1692 and 1721, killing hundreds.

In England, religious laws were very strict. Some groups wanted to leave and start new churches in the New World. In 1620, the Mayflower brought 102 pilgrims to the shores of what would become Massachusetts. In 1623, another explorer arrived. The Reverend William Blaxton (sometimes spelled Blackstone) also wanted to set up a religious settlement. To his surprise, the land he and the others had planned to live on was already occupied by another group of English settlers.

Although most of the other travelers returned to England, Blaxton remained, striking out to find land for himself. He built a cabin and planted an orchard on 800 empty acres on the western slope of the future Beacon Hill. The Reverend became the Boston area's first permanent European resident.

Within a few years, Puritans and Quakers immigrated to the New England area. From that point on, the region grew quickly. In 1630, Blaxton made arrangements with a group of Puritan settlers who wanted to move to the peninsula. Their leader, Isaac Johnson, named the new town Boston after his home in England. By the early 1700s, it had its first public school (the Boston Latin School), a mint (the Hull Mint) that produced the country's first paper money, a newspaper (*The Boston News-Letter*), and a printing press. The printing press was sponsored by the first institution of higher education in the English colonies, Harvard College, which was founded in 1636.

**The Old State House, built in 1713, is the oldest surviving public building in Boston and remains one of the oldest public buildings in the entire United States.**

## A Time of War

The second half of the eighteenth century was full of conflict and fighting for Boston. The Thirteen Colonies remained under England's control. That is not what they wanted. They had left Europe to find religious freedom, as well as a chance to start new lives. They wanted their own nation: the United States. England was not about to let them go that easily, however.

On March 22, 1765, Britain passed the Stamp Act. It placed a tax on all kinds of papers—from newspapers and legal documents to licenses and playing cards. Colonists were not happy. They had to pay the tax, but they had no say in how the money was used. This was known as "taxation without representation." Inspired, people from nine of the colonies convened a Stamp Act Congress and drafted a Declaration of Rights and Grievances, which they presented to the British. They demanded the Stamp Act be repealed. During this time, those most adamantly protesting the Stamp Act organized themselves into the "Sons of Liberty," a group that later included notables like Samuel Adams, Paul Revere, and Patrick Henry. The Stamp Act was finally repealed—but not until March 18, 1766. News of the repeal reached Boston in May, and they celebrated by ringing bells, firing guns, setting off fireworks, and lighting bonfires.

England was not finished with the colonies. In 1768, it sent troops to Boston to remind them that the British were still in control. Tensions increased and erupted on March 5, 1770. A fight broke out in front of Boston's Old State House. A group of people began hurling insults—and snowballs—at a "redcoat," or British soldier. Stones replaced the snowballs. Then clubs came out. Soldiers who came to support the British sentry ended up firing into the crowd. When the

**The site of the Boston Massacre, outside the Old State House, is marked with a memorial plaque and is one of the stops on the Freedom Trail.**

The Boston Tea Party Ships & Museum features interactive exhibits, historic artifacts, and replica sailing vessels to give you a peek back into the days leading up to the American Revolution.

fighting was over, five civilians were dead. Colonists called the melee the Boston Massacre.

Another famous conflict sparked by taxation and occupation occurred on December 16, 1773. The Sons of Liberty, in response to the Tea Act of May 10, 1773, disguised themselves, boarded East India Company ships, and dumped the 342 chests of tea in the shipment overboard. The damage done during the Boston Tea Party would be valued over $1.5 million in modern currency.

With these smaller protests and fights sparking up throughout Boston and beyond, it wouldn't be long before the British and the colonists were fully engaged in battle, with the colonists being led by General George Washington. On April 19, 1775, the Revolutionary War

The Bunker Hill Monument is a tall granite obelisk. Nearby is a bronze statue of Colonel William Prescott, who commanded patriot forces during the battle.

officially began. British troops faced local soldiers at Lexington and Concord, near Boston, and the first shot of the Revolution was fired. After this battle, the siege of Boston began. From April 1775 to March 1776, the Continental Army and British Army skirmished and raided back and forth over land access to the city. In the middle of the siege, on June 17, 1775, the Americans attempted to block the British at Bunker Hill. They were eventually forced to retreat back over the hill, leaving the British in control of the area. The British held the peninsula until March.

After months of small battles back and forth, on July 4, 1776, the colonists declared their independence from Britain. Boston remained an important strategic and symbolic location throughout the remaining eight years of the war. Finally, the British surrendered, signing the Treaty of Paris in September 1783 and freeing the colonies.

By this time, Boston was one of the largest cities in the United States, with a diverse population of about 15,000 people. Every one was now officially an American.

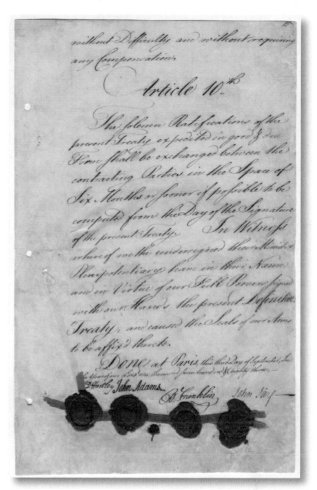

The Treaty of Paris was signed by John Adams, Benjamin Franklin, and John Jay for the United States. It was signed by David Hartley for Great Britain.

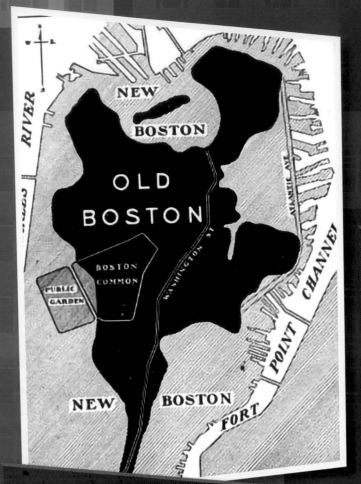

Above: Starting in the 1820s, Irish, Italian, and many other immigrants came to Boston to live and work to build the city. Immigrant Donald McKay created a shipyard in 1845 and for over 40 years produced ships that broke speed records.

After the Revolutionary War, Boston began to grow, both in population and by extending the land to create a new, wider shoreline. Right: The USS Constitution, also known as "Old Ironsides," is just one of the few amazing things to see and explore in Boston's Charlestown Navy Yard.

# Progress, Fire, and Flood

The Boston area was settled largely because of its location on the water. This water also made it a convenient location for shipping and manufacturing. In the 17th century, shipyards began to emerge along the city's waterfront in areas like the North End and Charlestown. They produced small fishing boats and large trading ships at first but began building warships during the Revolutionary War. The Edmund Hartt Shipyard was one of the most prominent in the industry, eventually building the famous USS Constitution, also known as "Old Ironsides," in 1797. This iconic ship played an important role in the history of the United States, most notably in the War of 1812. It is said to have earned its nickname from British cannonballs seemingly bouncing off the sturdy oak hull.

Because of its location, Boston continued to grow into the 19th century as a hub of manufacturing and shipping. During these years, fast and reliable clipper ships became integral to international shipping. Donald McKay's East Boston Shipyard was one of the top clipper ship builders in the world. Other industries in Boston grew alongside the shipyards. Textiles, shoes and other leather goods, heavy equipment and machinery, furniture, and paper products were all significant parts of Boston's early economic growth.

Boston was also well known in the food industry, particularly in brewing and chocolate-making. Bakers Chocolate Company, opened by Dr. James Baker and Irish immigrant John Hannon

**This advertising trading card shows the company's chocolate mills and packaging when the company was doing business as Walter Baker & Co.**

in the Dorchester neighborhood, was the first chocolate producer in the United States, selling solid baking chocolate bars. Because of the historic conflicts around tea taxation during the Revolution, grinding these bars to make drinking chocolate was very popular at the time. Hot chocolate was seen as a patriotic beverage to most Americans.

This period also saw huge growth in Boston's population. In the mid-1800's, the Great Famine in Ireland led to a massive wave of Irish people coming to Boston. Many of these immigrants worked as skilled shipbuilders or in the growing rail industry, which transported Boston-made goods and goods unloaded from foreign ships all over the Northeast. This Irish presence is apparent throughout the city. Boston's St. Patrick's Day Parade is the oldest in the country, traditional Irish dishes are huge parts of the local cuisine, and their NBA team, the Celtics, have Lucky the Leprechaun as a mascot.

Boston had also long been a haven for intellectuals, philosophers, and creatives. After the Revolution, many of these people shifted their focus to the abolitionist movement and its efforts to end slavery. Boston had long had a rich African American community and the African Meeting House, built in 1806 to serve as the African Baptist Church, was also a center for community gatherings and abolitionist activities. William Lloyd Garrison founded the New England Anti-Slavery Society there and it later became a meeting place for the New England Freedom Association, which was dedicated to helping freedom seekers on the Underground Railroad.

**Ralph Waldo Emerson was active in the Transcendentalism movement, a philosophy focused on independence, natural human goodness, and the divine experience in the everyday.**

Boston is also known to some as the birthplace of American literature. During this period, locals like Ralph Waldo Emerson, Nathaniel Hawthorne, Henry David Thoreau, Louisa May Alcott, and Henry Wadsworth Longfellow were creating classic, influential works that are still required learning in most schools across the country. Their books were published by Boston publishers and they made Boston a hub of culture and art.

The Boston of this time was thriving and crowded. Over 100,000 people were living there, and more were arriving every day. More and more homes and businesses were built. Miles of railroad track were laid to move people and goods at the roaring speed of 20 miles per hour.

Much of the city changed on the evening of November 9, 1872, when, in the basement of a dry goods warehouse, a small fire started. Soon, flames engulfed the building and spread. Although many

**The Boston and Lowell Railroad's North Station was one of the first in the United States.**

buildings were made of stone and brick, they had wooden window frames, trim, and roofs. The wood, combined with the narrowness of the streets, allowed the fire to race down the streets. It burned uncontrolled for 12 straight hours.

The fire department faced many challenges. The city's water mains were old. They had not been upgraded to deal with the city's growing population. Water supplies were limited. The fire trucks were pulled by horses. In a case of bad timing, most of the city's horses were ill, making them slow and clumsy. The Boston firefighters desperately telegraphed neighboring cities for help. However, because it was late, most telegraph offices were already closed.

The Great Boston Fire destroyed 65 acres of property. It burned down 776 buildings and did 73.5 million dollars' worth of damage (equivalent to almost $2 billion in 2023). At least 30 people died, including a dozen firefighters.

Rebuilding Boston happened almost immediately. Strict building codes and fire laws were put into place to keep the city safer and more fireproof. Regular fire inspections were required. The downtown area most damaged by the fire originally held rows of

**Standing at 496 feet tall, the Custom House Tower has 36 columns, each carved from a single piece of granite from nearby Quincy. The building is supported by 3,000 wood piles driven down to the bedrock.**

warehouses, small businesses, and elegant mansions. A number of larger businesses saw this burned land as the perfect chance to expand into downtown, creating Boston's first financial district.

Today, Boston's financial district is a fascinating mix of old and new, and is considered by many to be the heart of all of New England's banking and finance. The city's first skyscraper, the Boston Custom House Tower, was built from 1913 to 1915 and used the foundation from the original 1849 custom house. While the financial district has the historically famous Old South Meeting House, the organizing point for the Boston Tea Party protest in 1773, and the Bell in Hand Tavern, America's oldest tavern, it also has sparkling skyscrapers, banks, condos, and stores.

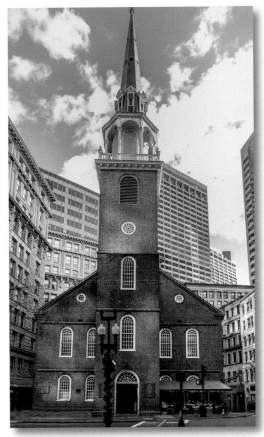

**The Old South Meeting House is one of a few historical buildings still standing alongside the flashier modern buildings of Boston's financial district.**

The years surrounding the fire saw other changes, as well. Boston saw even more population growth and cultural influence from other countries. Italian immigrants began arriving in Boston in large numbers in the late 1800s and early 1900s, contributing to the city's vibrant culinary scene, especially in Boston's historic North End neighborhood. The South Boston and Charlestown neighborhoods were still strongly Irish, but Russian Jewish immigrants began making the West End their home. Chinese immigrants also began to settle in Boston in the late 19th century, particularly in Boston's Chinatown. The neighborhoods began to develop into enclaves of ethnically distinct immigrants with unique and recognizable personalities and cultural events.

## A Ferocious Flood

On a mild January afternoon in 1919, Boston's North End was bustling. The city was full of sounds: the clopping of horses' hooves, the rumble of the elevated train, and the hum of countless conversations. In the background, the nearby Purity Distilling Company's huge metal tank groaned and moaned. No one paid any attention to it. The tank had been making those sounds ever since it had been built four years earlier. At 50 feet tall and 90 feet in diameter, the tank held 2.3 million gallons of molasses. It was to be used for making rum, ethanol, and munitions.

Suddenly, the air was filled with a terrifying metallic screech. The metal rivets holding the Purity Distilling Company's tank together gave way. They flew through the air like shrapnel. The sides of the tank tore open and a 25-foot-tall wave of molasses moving at 35 miles per hour swept over the North End. Buildings toppled or were pushed off their foundations. People were knocked off their feet and covered in a two- to three-foot layer of molasses.

Help arrived immediately. Police officers, firefighters, and more than one hundred sailors from the USS *Nantucket* rushed to pull

**In 1919, a flood of molasses destroyed buildings and claimed 21 lives.**

**Molasses is usually very slow so you might not think of it as dangerous. During the 1919 flood, however, an overwhelming volume of the thick liquid was released at unexpected speeds—turning it into a relentless sticky force pushing into the city.**

people and animals out of the muck. They had to move quickly. Cooling temperatures would harden the molasses.

Cleanup took weeks as mere soap and water was not enough to cut through the molasses. Instead, workers used saltwater from the nearby Atlantic Ocean.

The Great Molasses Flood killed 21 people. More than 150 were injured. The Purity Distilling Company was found at fault for not meeting safety standards when the tank was built. The steel plates on the tank were too thin to support the heavy molasses and not enough rivets were used. Because of this disaster, Boston's businesses were held to stricter safety codes and regular inspections.

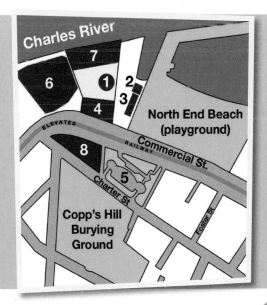

1. **Purity Distilling molasses tank**
2. **Firehouse 31 (heavy damage)**
3. **Paving department and police station**
4. **Purity offices (flattened)**
5. **Copp's Hill Terrace**
6. **Boston Gas Light Building (damaged)**
7. **Purity warehouse (mostly intact)**
8. **Residential area (where houses were flattened)**

Above: Irish immigrant Charles E. Logue designed Boston's immortal Fenway Park. The park is home to the "Green Monster"—a 37-foot-tall wooden wall. Left: Boston Symphony Hall began construction in 1899. The architects hired a Harvard physicist, Wallace Clement Sabine, to help with the shape of the walls, the placement of the seats, the angles for the stage, and the use of materials like felt to help produce the best sound.

# Modern Boston and The Big Dig

As Boston moved forward into the 20th century, the city continued to develop. Architecture and education boomed. Boston Symphony Hall opened in 1900 as the home of the world-famous Boston Symphony Orchestra, and Boston added many more beautiful art museums, studios, and music halls, an Opera House, and a Horticultural Hall. Boston's subway system and Logan International Airport were both completed and opened during these early decades.

This period saw many wealthy Bostonians supporting the arts. Isabella Stewart Gardner, for example, began collecting art in the late 1890s and dreamed of publicly exhibiting her collection. The museum opened on January 1, 1903, and became a haven for artists and education. The museum is perhaps best known, however, for a still-unsolved art heist that occurred on March 18, 1990. The two thieves disguised themselves as police officers and escaped with 13 pieces of art, including works by Vermeer, Rembrandt, and Degas. The stolen items were valued over $500 million and the mystery has never been solved.

An icon of Boston sports, Fenway Park, was built in 1912 to be the home of the Red Sox, one of the oldest Major League Baseball teams. They were founded in 1901 and have won nine World Series championships, most recently in 2018. They also, however, had one of the longest droughts in baseball history. Known as the "Curse of the Bambino," supposedly the team's inability to make the championships

**The Isabella Stewart Gardner Museum was the site of a still-unsolved art heist that occurred on March 18, 1990.**

stemmed from the sale of their star player, Babe Ruth, to longtime rival, the New York Yankees.

Sports would come to be very important to everyday Boston life over the next few decades. The Bruins, Boston's NHL team, was founded in 1924. They were the first American team in the NHL and won the Stanley Cup six times. Boston has an NBA team, the Celtics, which was founded in 1946. Since 1995, the Bruins and Celtics have shared TD Garden as their home arena.

## An Ambitious Project

It seemed like a good idea at the time.

As Boston grew, so did the city's traffic jams. By the late 1940s, it was clear that something needed to be done to streamline the long rows of traffic. In 1948, the city began building a six-lane elevated highway. It reached from Boston's downtown to its waterfront. In order to construct the highway, 1,000 buildings had to be torn down. More than 20,000 Bostonians had to move.

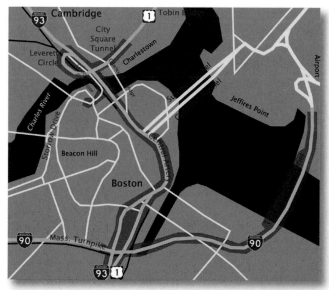

**Plans for the Big Dig (in pink) resulted in this new route with bridges and tunnels under or near existing highways.**

**Because of dirt relocated from the Big Dig, Spectacle Island, once a dumping ground for various city waste products, is now a lush, green visiting spot.**

The construction was finished in 1959. The highway was designed to handle about 75,000 vehicles every single day—which it did. However, by the 1990s, more than 190,000 vehicles were crossing it—or attempting to. The traffic was terrible. The Massachusetts Department of Transportation predicted eventual traffic jams of up to 16 hours a day. By the 1980s, city planners were discussing replacing it.

For several years, city planners and architects tried to figure out how to replace the elevated highway without having to shut it down in the process. At first, the city considered building a system of suspension bridges. In the end, they decided to go the opposite direction—they would build underground tunnels with expressways 8 to 14 lanes wide.

While the official name for the new project was the Central Artery/Tunnel Project, it quickly earned the nickname of the Big Dig. Construction began in 1991. Soon, the city realized just how difficult a goal it had set.

**A major challenge for the Big Dig was constructing all of the necessary tunnels. After all the dirt was excavated, the complicated construction process could begin.**

More than 16 million cubic yards of dirt had to be dug out. That was enough to fill a sports stadium all the way to the top—16 times! It required 541,000 truckloads to move away all that dirt, which was later used all over New England to fill in quarries, cover landfills, and convert former dump sites like nearby Spectacle Island. The project used so much reinforced steel that it could have wrapped around the entire planet at the equator.

The project's scope was so large that experts compared it to creating the Panama Canal or England's Chunnel. More than 5,000 people worked on it.

The city promised not to bother people during the construction. Utilities were not to be disturbed. Since people living in nearby apartments could not keep their windows open during the summer because of the noise, the city paid for their air conditioning and soundproof windows. Some people even got free firm mattresses to counteract the shaking from the nearby earthmoving equipment.

The Central Artery was finished in 2003. It had soared far past the predicted cost to $15 billion. This made it one of the most expensive construction projects in U.S. history. It took eight more years than planned to finish, thanks to a series of unexpected events. Blueprints

did not line up properly. Concrete was mixed improperly. At one point, ceilings collapsed. Then, near the South Station rail yards, the soil was so unstable, workers could not stand on it to work. To solve the problem, refrigerator units were brought in. They were used to freeze the ground so that work could continue.

**The cable-stayed Leonard P. Zakim Bunker Hill Memorial Bridge (the Zakim Bridge) carries ten lanes of traffic across the Charles River. It connects Cambridge and Boston.**

All the effort, time, and money had a huge impact. Commuting time was cut in half with the new expressways. Because traffic keeps moving, there are fewer emissions, so there is less air pollution. Boston's carbon monoxide levels dropped 12 percent once the Central Artery opened.

The Big Dig helped bring many more tourists to the city. This extra tourism improved the city's economy. In addition to the expressways, the city created more than 45 parks and public plazas where the elevated highways once ran. Instead of traffic jams, the area now has hundreds of trees and countless happy visitors.

Boston embraces the old while continuing to grow. Top: The Museum of Fine Arts hosts over one million visitors a year. Middle: Established in 1634, Boston Common is America's oldest public park. Bottom: The Old North Church was built in 1723 and is the oldest standing church in Boston.

# A Timeless City

Boston reflects the rich history of the past and the shining potential of the future. Memorials, plaques, statues, and historic buildings and sites are scattered throughout the city that once was the center for the fight for the country's independence.

One of Boston's most popular tourist attractions is the Freedom Trail. The tour winds for 2.5 miles through the city. It begins at Boston Common, where the first militia from the colonies trained to fight. Another stop is the Granary Burial Ground. Many patriots and war heroes are buried there, including Paul Revere and Samuel Adams. Tourists often spend extra time at Paul Revere's house and the Old North Church. On April 18, 1775, the church's sexton placed two lanterns in the steeple, kicking off the famous midnight ride of Paul Revere and the other riders who warned the Colonists of the British Army's movements.

Also popular is the city's Black Heritage Trail, which is operated by the Museum of African American History and the National Park Service. This self-guided audio tour is a 1.6-mile walk through the Beacon Hill neighborhoo. Many of the buildings are private residences, but some stops can be toured, like the influential African Meeting House and the Abiel Smith School.

Every stop on the Freedom Trail and the Black Heritage Trail is a glimpse into America's past.

**At 790 feet high, the John Hancock Tower is the tallest building in Boston. People on the upper floors used to get motion sickness when the building swayed in the wind. A tuned mass damper, which reduces vibrations, was installed on the 58th floor to help stabilize the building. This was the first TMD system to be used in a building.**

Boston honors its past, but it is also focused on its future. In July 2017, the city published its first citywide plan in 50 years, called "Imagine Boston 2030." Based on the input of more than 15,000 experts and residents, this plan describes how the city will change as the city reaches its 400th birthday and beyond. The city has continued to update the plan over the past few years.

Boston's population is only going to grow in the coming years. In 2023, its population is over 650,000. Experts predict it will reach 724,000

**The Franklin Park Zoo is part of the Emerald Necklace, which is a 1,100-acre chain of parks and waterways that winds through Boston and Brookline. Landscape architect Frederick Law Olmstead designed it to appear as a piece of jewelry around the "neck" of the Boston peninsula.**

by 2030 and 801,000 by 2050. The city plans to build thousands more apartments, homes, and condos. It will also add hotels, restaurants, supermarkets, shops, and offices. Many of these homes and businesses will be housed in soaring skyscrapers.

Boston also plans to make the city more "green," or eco-friendly. The plan is to create more open spaces and use fewer fossil fuels. The plan also calls for more flood protection at the waterfront, to provide safety from the rising water levels predicted to occur because of climate change.

Whether walking through Boston to experience a taste of the past or strolling through to see how the future might change this great city, visitors are sure to be amazed. The city is a continuing work in progress. It reaches for new possibilities while standing on the shoulders of some of the nation's most important moments in history.

# Chronology

**BCE**

**2400**  Native Americans are living on Shawmut.

**1600**  More than 100,000 Algonquin live throughout the area that will one day be called New England.

**CE**

**1614**  Captain John Smith explores the coast of what he calls New England.

**1617**  Europeans bring the disease smallpox to New England. It devastates the Native American population there, killing almost 90% of their population.

**1620**  The Mayflower brings 102 passengers from England to Massachusetts. These pilgrims want to start a new church in the New World.

**1623**  The Reverend William Blaxton arrives from England to set up a religious settlement. He settles on Beacon Hill.

**1630**  The town of Boston is officially created.

**1636**  Harvard College is founded.

**1765**  The British pass the Stamp Act, which taxes colonists for using paper. The tax is repealed the following March.

**1770**  During the Boston Massacre, Boston patriots taunt British troops, who fire back at the crowd. Five civilians are killed.

**1773**  The Boston Tea Party protest occurs.

**1775**  The Revolutionary War begins on April 19 at the Battle of Concord, near Boston. Boston is under siege and the Battle of Bunker Hill occurs very close to the city.

**1776**  Delegates from the Thirteen Colonies sign the Declaration of Independence. On July 18, Bostonians gather at the Old State House to hear the document read aloud.

**1783**  The British surrender, and the Treaty of Paris ends the Revolutionary War.

**1861**  The Massachusetts Institute of Technology is established.

**1872**  A fire razes hundreds of buildings in downtown Boston. The city will rebuild using stricter building codes and fire laws.

**1897**  The first Boston Marathon is run in April.

**1901**  Boston Red Sox founded.

**1915**  The city's first skyscraper, the Boston Custom House Tower, is completed.

**1919**  In January, a huge tank holding 2.3 million gallons of molasses bursts, covering several city blocks and claiming the lives of 21 people.

**1948**  Boston begins building an elevated highway designed to relieve traffic jams. It will be completed in 1959.

# Chronology

**1976**  John Hancock Tower built. It would later feature the first use of a tuned mass damper in a building.

**1993**  Work on the Big Dig begins.

**2007**  The Big Dig is completed. Its total cost is $15 billion.

**2013**  Terrorists bomb the Boston Marathon. Three people die and more than 300 are injured. The Red Sox win the World Series, their third win since 2004 and their first series win at Fenway Park since 1918.

**2017**  A report called "Imagine Boston 2030" outlines plans for how Boston will grow over the next few decades.

**2021**  Michelle Wu becomes the first woman elected as Mayor of Boston.

## Books

Baby Professor. What Happened at the Boston Massacre? Newark, DE: Baby Professor Books, 2017.

Petersen, Justin. Boston Marathon (World's Greatest Sporting Events). Oakland, CA: Scobre Educational, 2015.

Shea, Therese. The Boston Massacre (What You Didn't Know about History). New York: Gareth Stevens, 2014.

Winters, Kay. Colonial Voices: Hear Them Speak: The Outbreak of the Boston Tea Party Told from Multiple Points of View. New York: Puffin Books, 2015.

Yee, Kristina, and Frances Poletti. The Girl Who Ran: Bobbi Gibb, The First Woman to Run the Boston Marathon. Seattle, WA: Compendium Inc., 2017

## Works Consulted

Acitelli, Tom. "12 Boston Developments Set to Transform the City." Boston Curbed. May 14, 2017. https://boston.curbed.com/maps/boston-developments-new-2017

Andres, Evan. "The Great Molasses Flood of 1919." History.com. January 13, 2017. https://www.history.com/news/the-great-molasses-flood-of-1919

Brooke, Rebecca Beatrice. History of Massachusetts. 2011–2023. https://historyofmassa-chusetts.org

Enwemeka, Zeninjor. "Plan Provides Road Map for What Boston Should Look Like in 2030." WBUR. July 11, 2017. https://www.wbur.org/bostonomix/2017/07/11/imagine-boston-2030-final-plan

# Further Reading

Flint, Anthony. "10 Years Later, Did the Big Dig Deliver?" *The Boston Globe*, December 29, 2015. https://www.bostonglobe.com/magazine/2015/12/29/years-later-did-big-dig-deliver/tSb8PIMS4QJUETsMpA7SpI/story.html

Gelinas, Nicole. "Lessons of Boston's Big Dig." City Journal. Autumn 2007. https://www.city-journal.org/article/lessons-of-bostons-big-dig

"Globe Coverage of the First Boston Marathon." Boston.com. April 20, 1897. http://archive.boston.com/marathon/history/1897_globe.htm

Herwick, Edgar. "From 'Beantown' to 'The Hub,' How Did Boston Earn Its Nicknames?" WGBH News, August 30, 2017. https://news.wgbh.org/2017/08/30/local-news/beantown-hub-how-did-boston-earn-its-nicknames

Mancini, Mark. "Why Is Boston Called 'Beantown'?" Mental Floss. May 16, 2014. https://mentalfloss.com/article/56690/why-boston-called-beantown

Massachusetts Department of Transportation. "The Big Dig." Undated. https://www.mass.gov/the-big-dig

"Recap of the First Boston Marathon (1897)." Click Americana. Undated. https://clickamericana.com/media/newspapers/recap-of-the-first-boston-marathon-1897

Stanly, Robert. "The Great Molasses Flood." New England.com January 15, 2018. https://newengland.com/yankee/history/great-molasses-flood/

## On the Internet

Boston Athletic Association's The Boston Marathon: Bring the Kids
https://www.baa.org/races/10k/event-information/bring-the-kids.aspx

Ducksters: The Boston Tea Party
https://www.ducksters.com/history/boston_tea_party.php

Ducksters: Massachusetts State History
https://www.ducksters.com/geography/us_states/massachusetts_history.php

Social Studies for Kids: Boston Marathon Winners
https://www.socialstudiesforkids.com/articles/sports/bostonmarathon-famous.htm

# Glossary

**Abenaki** (ah-beh-NAH-kee)—A member of a group of Native Americans who lived in northern New England; the language of the Abenaki.

**carbon monoxide** (KAR-bin muh-NOK-syd)—A colorless, odorless gas that contributes to air pollution.

**civilian** (sih-VIL-yin)—A person who is not in the military.

**colonist** (KAH-luh-nist)—A person who lives in a colony, which is any area outside the country that governs it.

**commute** (kuh-MYOOT)—To travel on a regular route to and from work.

**eco-friendly** (EE-koh FREND-lee)—Not harmful to the environment.

**economy** (ee-KAH-nuh-mee)—The exchange of goods and services in a community.

**emissions** (ee-MIH-shuns)—Energy or materials released after a chemical process.

**epidemic** (eh-pih-DEH-mik)—Widespread; affecting many people.

**expedition** (ek-speh-DIH-shun)—An organized trip.

**fossil fuels** (FAH-sul fyoolz)—Materials such as coal, gas, and oil that are mined from the earth and burned for energy.

**grueling** (GROO-ling)—Extremely difficult and tiring.

**massacre** (MAS-ih-kur)—The deliberate killing of many people.

**melee** (MEH-lay)—A confused fight.

**mint** (MINT)—A place that prints or molds currency (money).

**mitigation** (mih-tih-GAY-shun)—The process of making something less severe or damaging.

**munitions** (myoo-NIH-shunz)—Explosive materials used as weapons.

**peninsula** (peh-NIN-soo-luh)—A piece of land that projects into water.

**repeal** (ree-PEEL)—To undo (a law).

**rivet** (RIH-vet)—A short metal fastener with a head on each end.

**smallpox** (SMALL-poks)—A deadly disease that infects the skin.

# Index